The

Enlightened

WOMAN

Inspiration and Reflections to Rediscover the Joy of Being You in Midlife and Beyond

REV. DR. KELLIE V. HAYES

Publisher: Enlightened Woman Enterprises, LLC

Editor: Janelle Harris-Dixon, The Write or Die Chick

Cover Design: Christian D. Belton, CB Creates, LLC

Cover Photo: Jackie Hicks, Fond Memories Photography

Make-up: Letitia Thornhill, LET Beauty

Hayes, Kellie V

1. Women in Midlife 2. African American Women in Midlife
3. Women's Empowerment 4. Women's Spiritual Enlightenment
5. Women in transition 6. Christian Inspirational
7. Motivational Self-help

ISBN 978-0-578-62342-9
Library of Congress No. - 2020911221

www.enlightenedwoman.global

Enlightened Woman
ENTERPRISES, LLC

Praises for The Enlightened Woman...

"Dr. Hayes has shown us the way to let go of self-limiting beliefs that have kept us from embracing our true worth and beauty. Her sound spiritual wisdom and thought-provoking questions challenge us to be open to a higher level of understanding and truth. Every page is packed with inspiration reminding us that every stage of our lives is a gift to be embraced. And as we persevere through the inevitable challenges, we will rediscover the joy of becoming our authentic selves."

Minister Natalie Brown Rudd, author of *Stormy Weather: Twenty-five Lessons Learned While Weathering the Storms of Life*

"When reading one's obituary there's a standard entry regardless of race, age, gender or cause of death. It's the date of birth and the date of death. More resonant is the "dash" between those two dates that contains many stories, lessons, and pivotal moments. How we "work the middle," determines our legacy and how we will be remembered. Some may think my illustration is morbid. I prefer to call it "sounding the alarm" to women "transitioning through midlife" to live your best life every day. Find some sweetness daily. Make the moments between the hot flashes matter (girl, shut up LOL). We each have the power and get to choose how we negotiate our dash. The not so pleasant moments can be transmuted into significance, fulfillment, wisdom, and deep meaning. Intention determines impact. *The Enlightened Woman: Inspiration and Reflections to Rediscover the Joy of Being You in Midlife and Beyond,* by Kellie Hayes, is a must read for every woman approaching, currently in or coming out of midlife. After you read it, then leave the light on for another woman. Share this book along with your lessons. We are enlightened to elevate others. *The best is yet to come!*

Dr. Vikki Johnson
Chaplain, Speaker, Author,
& Creator, Soul Wealth®
www.vikkijohnson.com

"The permission that has been granted in this book for women to embrace the inevitable reality of navigating through their midlife journey is necessary and on point. Throughout the writing of Dr. Kellie Hayes' book, *The Enlightened Woman,* you realize that Dr. Kellie took time to go inward and what has emerged is the charge to embrace inward and outward positive and productive change for the here and now, and the future. Receive the insight, wisdom, and direction from one who has done the work needed and reminds us that midlife is more than hot flashes and sleepless nights. It is a God opportunity that can be an inspirational and empowering time in a woman's life. Read, reflect, enjoy, and step into your destiny!"

Rev. Dr. Jo Ann Browning
Co-Pastor
Ebenezer A.M.E. Church
Fort Washington, Md.

"*The Enlightened Woman* is not just another book to read; it is an experience to have, for women as they navigate through midlife and beyond. Dr. Kellie shares a rare, raw, and real look at the challenges and triumphs she faced on this "tumultuous journey" (her words) to uncover her unsanitized truth. The book is indeed a road map with action steps for those who are willing to do the work. If that's you, then you will come through on the other side with grace and dignity, living and celebrating your authentic self."

Dr. Gloria Miller Perrin
Associate Pastor
First Baptist Church of Glenarden
Author, *Raising the Bar: Building Authentic Relationships*

"In this unprecedented time of global and national crises, Dr. Kellie Hayes offers a candid, introspective view of her midlife journey. Kellie presents this pivotal moment initially as one of dread and despair, yet it ultimately leads her to an empowering road of self-identity and self-confidence. *The Enlightened Woman* is a clarion call for women to keep moving forward with zeal and excitement, as God has so much in store at this juncture that you don't want to miss—your latter will be greater. With clarity, wisdom, humor, and action steps, Kellie will help you become more bold and courageous, grounded, happier, and free to be the woman He created you to be. It's time for all of us to be *Enlightened* with such a great Word from a woman of God and open our minds to receive a shift in perspective to this so-called midlife crisis."

Kim A. Rouse
CEO & IP Visionary
Covenant Consulting LLC

Dedication

To the amazingly brilliant tribe of women in my life who shaped me and created a path for me.

Especially Lula Mae Brown, better known as Big Mama, my prayer warrior and protector. Luretha Grills my MaDear, the one who sacrificed to bring me into the Earth and made sure I had everything I needed. She's still my rock.

Acknowledgments

No one does anything on their own and gratefully I am no exception. *The Enlightened Woman* is the fruit of divine intervention and sacred relationships. I was raised on the adage that good manners will take you far, and this includes saying thank you. I must acknowledge and say thank you to those who made my life, and dreams possible. Those who created the environment for me to grow, evolve and embrace my calling and freedom.

It is in God I live, move and have my being. I am eternally grateful for my relationship with God, She is my creative source.

My muse, twin-flame and partner in love and life, Dr. Harold B. Hayes, Jr., better known as "honey." Your love, presence and encouragement are life-giving. Your existence makes the world better. Thank you for the constant nudge to go after my heart's desire and finish this book.

Thank you to my Auntie Tribe: Ora Dee, Bertha Lee, Annie Bernice, Margaret Ann and Gwendolyn. They have always been my fierce advocates and ardent supporters. Thanks to my ever supportive and super gifted sister-cousins, Sonya and Natalie, my inspiration and legacy partners. We are Big Mama's girls living the dream.

Thank you to my mother-in-love Pearline Barfield Hayes, strength and faith personified. My sister-in-love, Elder Darlene Belton, grace and resilience personified. My amazing nieces, Dani, Chrissy and Pearl, the Belton Beauties. Thanks for welcoming me into the family.

I am so very grateful for my spiritual mother, the Rev. Dr. JoAnn Browning. Your love for God is evident. Your heart and compassion for God's people is a balm to our souls. Having you as an example has been priceless. Thank you for seeing my unique anointing and calling. You nurtured it then and still do.

My daughters, Shante Venice and Shannon Kellene. My gifts and grace from God. I'm grateful to have been the vessel to birth such powerful women. My granddaughters, Tehila Brittany Jade and Daria Patricia Jo. My brilliant hope for the future and impact of women on the Earth.

To the team who made it happen. Janelle Harris-Dixon, The Write or Die Chick, editor extraordinaire. Your expertise is invaluable. Thank you for helping me make something beautiful with words. Christian Darlene Belton, CEO of CB Creates. Thank you for making my creativity a reality. The world is your canvas. Sandra Mizell Chaney who sat down with me in a Panera Bread to hear my idea years ago. Thank you for planting the seed, confirming the idea and offering my first blueprint. My book coach, Kim and her team. Your editorial prowess and eye are awesome. Thanks for stepping in and getting me across the finish line with excellence and a wonderful spirit.

To the inaugural Serenity Experience Sisters of 2019 for reading the first draft, being so encouraging and believing in the vision. It was an honor to see you rediscover your joy.

Thank you to my OSP Sisters, my #Equal Sisterhood and my Exhale sisters. My safe and sacred spaces where love abounds, tears are allowed and grace is given freely.

Thank you to the Rev. Renita Weems, Ph.D., your scholarly work, fierce wit and womanist agency mentored me from afar. My spiritual mother, Dr. Joann Browning exposed me to many great women, and you are one. I was grateful to finally meet you. On subsequent encounters I would feel the need to reintroduce myself, and you would embrace me with the remark "I know who you are." That embrace catapulted me on my own journey of self-actualization. I often quote your work, especially the sentiment that "we are thinking women of faith." Indeed we are.

Contents

Introduction

An Invitation to the Journey

My joy isn't a shield from the vicissitudes of life. It is my hope,
light, and anchor in the midst of them."
—Dr. Kellie V. Hayes

I knew I wasn't the only one. I'd heard and read horror stories about hot flashes, weight gain, health crises, empty nest syndrome, depression and marital trauma. Now, I had to face these same realities as my own mind and body weren't cooperating. My children noticed my incessant fanning and constantly asked me if I was having a hot flash.

Now I know why Claire Huxtable put her head in the freezer! My girlfriends and I lamented and laughed about adventuring through "the change." I generally laugh to keep from crying, but I still cried anyway. My husband couldn't relate. He thought I was overreacting until he saw my glasses steam up one day during a moment of internal combustion.

Deeper than that was an inward upheaval and an emotional tug of war. My soul and spirit were thirsty. I shuffled between feeling anger, malaise and panic. I thought, *what's going on* ? I needed answers. As a voracious reader, I searched for resources and information about women like me—proud African-American women. I found there was a dearth of research about our menopausal experience. I'm grateful for the few resources available, but most were dated back to 2003 or earlier. During my search, I also found an academic article about urban women in midlife. I was initially elated, only to find out that it had been written by two white women. What the hell? Why aren't we writing our own stories? I should have known when I saw the word "urban."

Here's the kicker. My life is far from horrible. I have an amazing husband, loving adult children, two beautiful granddaughters, a couple of degrees, opportunities to exercise my gifts and skills, and a circle of family and friends. Yet none of that precluded me from hitting a wall and experiencing a midlife shift. When I started having thoughts of walking away from it all, I knew it was time to do something. But what?

In those uncertain periods I still had my relationship with God. The Holy Spirit wooed me into a season of spiritual renovation. That's what midlife is—a renovation. You don't get rid of the foundation because that's still solid. You just demolish the walls and ceilings that need to come down. You rebuild and update. For five months, I went on an inward, sometimes painful journey of revelations that allowed me to rediscover myself and my joy.

I'm now on assignment to be a light and shed some light for other women. No matter where you are on your own journey, you're not alone. It's worth going through your renovation. The process will ultimately lead you to knowing yourself, loving yourself, and sharing yourself with wisdom and grace. As a result of my inward journey I declare that I am an enlightened woman!

"The kind of beauty I want most is the hard-to-get kind.
That comes from within - strength, courage and dignity"
—*Ruby Dee*

In the midlife season and beyond, it's vital that we don't give into the crisis and chaos that abound when this inevitable transformation takes over our psyches and bodies. You have two options: retreat from the upheaval or master it. This is your opportunity for a radical reset. Transform the narrative of midlife and celebrate the madness and magnificence of coming into your own. You're giving birth to your divine self.

We are part of the sacred sisterhood of women in midlife so it's time that we rediscover the joy of our uniqueness. Your courageous "yes" and your surrender to this season of life will yield new confidence and vitality. Embrace your beauty and brilliance. Allow yourself to be exposed to new experiences and explore the depths of your soul. Expand your mind and your spirit will evolve. Your renewed life is calling, waiting to be lived. I hope these inspirations and revelations free you to enjoy this inevitable journey as you rediscover the joy of being you.

The Enlightened Woman's

Midlife Manifesto

I am giving birth to myself. I am rising to the occasion of becoming me. All that I am is one glorious reflection of God. I am no longer afraid to embrace my pain because it has been transformed into power. My soul is too beautiful to live with regret, because regret does not serve me well. I'm not too full to learn until there is no more learning, just a knowing. I am a spark of God, She exists in every fiber of my being.

I am an enlightened woman led by the light of wisdom. I am freedom. It became mine when I realized it had always been there. I exude the confidence of the broken and cherish my tears as diamonds. I earned every one of them. They are the crown of the redeemed.

I am an enlightened woman. My shine cannot be diminished. It comes from within. When life is dark, it's only because that light has been covered. I choose to be kind to myself and uncover the light. I invite you to uncover yours too. We shine brightest together.

REFLECTIONS FROM AN ENLIGHTENED WOMAN

CHAPTER 1

Identity Crisis

"Once you know who you are, you don't have
to worry anymore."
— *Nikki Giovanni*

Who am I? Where Am I? Who took my life? These questions and more are vying for answers. Nothing causes an identity crisis like getting to midlife. I thought adolescence was bad. The periods and pads and tampon crisis followed by the full-on please-don't-let-it-leak-through-my-clothes-in-class-or-gym hysteria. The longing for the you know who of the moment to like you, all while trying to figure out what to do with your hair, skin and teeth, not to mention the daily wardrobe emergencies.

How about those grown-ish years when every decision you made was of earth- shattering proportion: What will they think if I do this? Birth control or "rubbers," or should I do it at all? Which career is going to make me the most money? Wait, I have to pay that bill too? Becoming an adult woman was not all it was cracked up to be, and nobody offered a class or handbook on being grown.

Dreams deferred. Hopes dashed. Wins and losses. Beginnings and endings. Accomplishments and gains—weight that is! Relationships, marriage(s), children, rent, mortgages, and all not necessarily in that order, if at all. Life can roll into one great big blur. Where did the time go? No matter how great, grand, or pitiful you think your life is, one day you'll wake up and say, "Who the hell is that woman in the mirror?"

If you haven't already asked these questions, trust me. You will. Welcome to the club. The illustrious sorority of women rediscovering the joy of being and living life on our own terms. Growing through it, not just going through it. Join me on this journey as we reflect on the transitions and transformation that can occur as we embrace the inevitable—the second half of life.

CHAPTER 2

My Way Back

*"And the day came when the risk to remain tight in a bud
was more painful than the risk it took to blossom."*
— Anais Nin

I thought I knew who I was. Yet something strange happened when I hit the big 5-0. I began to question everything. Why was I doing what I was doing? Where were the fruits of my labor? Had I accomplished anything? Where did the time go? It seemed that I looked up and 15 years had passed by and it felt like I had been treading water, going no-where.

I started paying attention to the passing of not just years, but days, and even minutes. I was having trouble focusing and making it beyond the first item on my daily to-do list. I looked around the landscape of my life and realized how small my surroundings had become.

The death of strangers particularly unnerved me. I mean, it's not as if people had not been dying all around me before. For some reason, each death became personal. I could see myself in their demise, afraid that I'd leave the Earth before I was fulfilled. My temper and patience became short. I felt like I was walking around in a perpetual fog. I couldn't remember "ish." Yes, I started cussing more. Imagine that, a cussing preacher. I felt lost in my own life and body. I couldn't put my finger on it. It was a level of disequilibrium that I hadn't felt before.

I thought to myself, *maybe I can escape*. But escape to where? And to do what? That's when the other stiletto dropped—I didn't think I was qualified to do anything else. Well, it is what it is. I decided to suck it up and be content. Then something rose up within me and I said, in my best Whitney Houston voice, "Hell to the naw! It's time to fight for your life and practice what you preach!"

Oddly enough, with all of the mental, emotional and physical dust-up happening, apparently my spirit was yet alive. Maybe God heard my constant prayers and cries of "Please help me." It turned out the madness was my true self saying, "Come back home." You can't be yourself and someone else at the same time. You can't meet everyone else's needs and expectations, and neglect your own without losing your soul. I had lost myself and wandered far from my true north and didn't even know it. Thankfully, my spirit did. She alerted me that it was time for a change, a transformation, and fighting for our survival would require a spiritual journey.

"I'm letting myself go and getting myself back."
— *Carleen Brice*

That's when it hit me that it's not about a new career, body, hair color, house or husband/man. It's about a new you. If after you've done the work of coming home to yourself and then decide you need a new career, body, hair color, house or husband/man, you'd better be ready to own and stand in it. You have to be clear about what you need in order to be whole because everybody in your life is not concerned about your wholeness. They're only concerned about how you can meet their needs. They will not be happy with your new found self-awareness.

Be careful as some will do everything in their power to guilt you back into compliance. That doesn't mean they don't love you, it just means you need to love yourself more and *show* them how to love you. Believe me, after you come through your season of introspection, release, and renewal, you won't care as much about what they think anyway. This is one of the best perks of midlife. Your brain rewires and says, "You're on a mission for yourself, not everyone else."

You must get quiet so you can hear your own voice and learn to trust her. Know what you want and what you like. What thoughts, beliefs, practices or people are you willing to let go of to gain a sense of worth and peace? What makes you smile, laugh and cry? What makes you feel like you're floating on air?

Once you know, go do that and lots of it. It's a matter of life or death. Choose life—yours.

My journey began in stages. Restlessness and questioning. Failures and reality checks. Health scares. Resignation and then the fight to be reborn. I heeded the Spirit's call and began to consistently and intentionally meditate and pray about my life to ask for guidance. In five months of grace and focused consecration, I listened for my voice. I didn't find it all at once. A book here, an article there, a song here, a conversation there. A revelation here, and a chain broken there. It was an arduous journey that gave way to a new found glory of self-acceptance and confidence. I embraced my divine power and acknowledge that I am wonderful and worthy. It's a daily process. I'm still evolving, but I've found my way back to me. So can you.

CHAPTER 3

Celebrate Yourself

"Be cheerful with joyous celebration in every season of your life. Let joy overflow, for you are united with the Anointed One."
— *Philippians 4:4 (TPT)*

Stop waiting for something special to happen to celebrate yourself. Your divine existence is worthy of a celebration. The angels rejoiced when God was knitting you in your mother's womb. Neither the circumstances of your birth nor the context of your upbringing diminishes the holiness of your presence on the Earth.

Prolonged seasons of suffering and struggle can alter your brain to operate in constant survival mode. You have to fight to rise above that. Get help and go to therapy again and again. Choose life. Find a tribe you can confide in that will hold you in a safe place and make you accountable to better choices. If you can't change the circumstances, ask for divine help but refuse to make struggle your identity. When you come out—or even in the midst, celebrate your strength and power to manage it. Give yourself credit for not giving up or giving in. Don't beat yourself up if you did give in for a season, honor yourself for getting back in the game. Small steps are worth celebrating.

I received my doctorate of ministry in May 2019. It took four months for me to actually realize, "Oh my God, I just received my doctorate of ministry!" That may be strange to you, but I had to put myself in a mindset to manage nearly four years of reading and writing, wife-ing and mothering and grandmothering and pastoring and preaching and teaching and daughtering and friending and planning and working and struggling financially and counseling and marrying and burying and getting sick and getting well and helping loved ones who were getting sick and getting well and mourning some who died and juggling life in all of its general complexity.

It was enormous and I cried at the impossibility. *Girl, you did it*, I told myself. With support and prayers, but you did it. You are capable. Did I mention that I did it through the hot flashes and brain fog and wardrobe crises from midlife metabolism shut down? Then there was the fatigue and the meltdowns and temper tantrums and the "why the hell am I doing this?" self-talk. You get my point. Sometimes we're so in the thick of the battle that when it's over, we don't know how to divorce ourselves from that existence.

I realized that I have more to celebrate than I do to lament. I believe we need to do them both. Once you know yourself you can fully celebrate yourself. I'm beautiful and compassionate. I'm intuitive and discerning. I'm a mystic, spiritual teacher, and carrier of the good news of Christ and the abundant life. I'm wise and funny and creative and I love my family and friends. I'm a wonderful wife—just ask my husband of 35 years.

I'm contemplative and enjoy my own company. I tend toward melancholy but I can party with the best of them. I'm a work in progress, but I accept myself even now. I love the sunshine and a good thunderstorm. I love to curl up with a good book by a fireplace in a snowstorm. I love adventure and life is the greatest of them all.

Now it's your turn. Look back over your life—heck, maybe even just this past week. I'm sure you have something to be thankful for and acknowledge. Let's celebrate each other. Take a deep breath in and let it out. You are breathing. That alone is a reason to celebrate.

Your Life is a Movement

Stop waiting for something extraordinary to happen in your life. You are the extraordinary happening. When you go to a symphony and listen to a beautiful piece, you realize at the end, what you just heard was only a portion of a larger composition. It's followed by another. Then another. Then another. Then another, each a completely distinctive movement.

Just like a classical piece of music, you're part of a grand composition written by the Master Composer who knows how many movements it will take to complete the masterpiece that is your life. You have your own key, rhythm, and themes. Without you, the grand symphony won't be complete. The beauty of your life, in all of its magnificent messiness, may seem like chaos to you. But it's the sound of sweet music to the Creator. Don't fret over this movement in your life. The Master Composer isn't finished with you yet. Your life is an answered prayer, an intentional thought, and a movement in the grand composition called life. Your life notes matter.

CHAPTER 4

Midlife Crossroads: The Death Of An Unexamined Life

*"We can act from our power instead of our weakness
anytime we choose."*
— Susan Taylor

We should all be grateful for hindsight. Life's circumstances make so much more sense when we're looking in the rear-view mirror, ergo the saying, "hindsight is 20/20." Things become abundantly clear when we have the benefit of time and added wisdom. When we're in the thick of a situation, it's hard to make sense of what's happening, especially if it's painful or involves loss. We somehow manage to forge ahead without taking time to acknowledge—let alone heal from the traumatic experiences in our lives. We need to take a good long hard look at them in order to benefit and learn from them. Socrates, one of the great Greek philosophers stated, "An unexamined life is not worth living." I encourage you to take a serious inventory and reevaluation of your life to help you make this next chapter worth its weight in gold.

As Black women in America, we have the unenviable charge of living at the intersection of gender and race. It makes our lives even more challenging. Add to the mix the lingering atrocities of slavery in our collective consciousness, and the fact that we have some level of rationality and success is a miracle. We've been dubbed "strong" and "invincible." We've been labeled "long-suffering" and worn "ride or die" as a badge of honor. We are stereotyped as "angry" and often admonished to "smile."

A Black man once told me, "You're pretty for a dark-skinned woman." I just glared at him too incredulously shocked and hurt to speak. He may have taken my silence for rudeness, but I didn't care. His colorism made him both the rude and ignorant one. Who made him the arbiter of beauty? That kind of daily injustice, coupled with micro and macro-aggressions against our humanity are enough to send us into prolonged psychological instability. For many of us, it has. Others just can't see it because you don't show it. We've managed to live decent lives and gained some level of success, but a gnawing, longing for something better lingers.

The truth is many of us are living in quiet desperation. We've put our hope in others to make our lives worthwhile and seem to be chasing a phantom carrot on the end of a constantly moving string just beyond our reach. We want to be accepted and loved for who we are. We're told all we have to do is conform, fit in, acquiesce, and work hard. In reality, we're hoping no one comes behind the curtain to discover our Wizard of Oz survival trickery.

> *"Midlife and menopause, it's a rite of passage, it's a time of emotional and spiritual transformation. As our bodies and minds prepare for our later years, many women become more assertive, self-confident, and in touch with their own needs and wants, and less interested in pleasing others."*
> *—Marilyn Hughes Gaston, M.D. and*
> *Gayle K. Porter, Psy. D.*

When midlife hits, it's as if our souls cross an invisible barrier. Our bullsh**t meter explodes and we have absolutely no more tolerance for nonsense. For some women, it happens gradually. For others, it's immediate and sudden because they realize they no longer have the time or energy to pretend. They're not willing to live a lie. It's time to make decisions, evaluate attachments, and assess relationships. They wonder, "Do I want to continue living my life this way?"

An unexamined life is an inauthentic life. Midlife is a crossroad, the intersection of your past life and the possibility of becoming your truest self. If you don't look within to determine the extent of your complicity in your own unhappiness, you'll never be free. Becoming self-aware means reclaiming your power. Contemplating and reflecting on the root causes of your pain helps you acknowledge it and empowers you to release victim consciousness. It restores your power of choice. You get to choose who you want to be and who has the privilege of basking in your love and wisdom. When you rediscover and embrace your authentic self, you take the next step in your path to becoming. Authenticity is freedom. It means no more hiding. It means finding your voice and using it.

The Creator implemented this midlife rite of passage to align everything within you. Your brain is rewiring for the next season and chapter of your life. Your body is shifting its purpose. Your spirit is longing to reach the heights of knowing and being known by God.

Look back and own every mistake and failure you've experienced. Embrace every disappointment and loss. Cry, grieve, sigh, scream. Find joy and pride in every accomplishment. Rejoice over every time you got back up and every time you gave love a chance. Acknowledge every opportunity, both missed and taken. Embrace your own super-shero powers. Welcome it all as the bridge of transformation into the woman you are now. Look her right in the eye and love her.

Flow In Your Rhythm

It's time to get your mojo back. If *Stella* did it, so can you. Stop being so careful. Quit worrying about what people will think—you can't control that anyway. Give yourself permission to be happy, to be free, to sleep late, to dance wildly, to laugh until you cry, and your side hurts. Let go and say exactly what you feel and how you feel it. Apologize later if necessary, or not. Stop second-guessing your intelligence and wisdom. Know the voice of the Divine and obey Her. She is you.

You don't need a man to "mansplain" what God meant. Tell your grown-ass children your time belongs to you and they must ask you first before coming over to your house, entering your space, or committing you, your time and your money to the advancement of their lives. Give it a try.

Wear whatever fits you, without regard to age limits. Fire the fashion police. Besides, you're the only one who has to manage the fallout. Show some cleavage and leg. Let the naysayers deal with their issues of appropriateness. Beat your face, go make-up-less, or do anything in-between. Wear your hair short or long, purple or blue, gray or blond. Rock a wig, extensions or go completely bald. India.Arie said it best, "you are not your hair." Your true beauty is within and the greatest accessory is the gen-uine smile that emanates from the joy of being you.

If you have the money and don't have to go into debt to do it, go ahead and tighten, lift, suck, nip and tuck any part of your body you want to tweak or change. Even get your vagina—or whatever you like to call her—rejuvenated. Dye your gray pu-bic hairs red, black or any color you desire. Shave it all off, get a landing strip, "vajazzle" it! As long as it's from a pure place of improvement and fun, and you're not trying to prove anything to anybody for any reason. Why not go for it?

Go to a new restaurant and eat something different. Learn a new language. Read or listen to a new book every month or, every other month, or at the very least, during the summer. Have a conversation with a stranger at a bar. Go on solo trips to the movies, out to eat or on an overdue vacation. Travel with a club or some girlfriends. Take a class just for the fun of it. Teach a class just for the fun of it. But if they want to pay you, by all means, take the money!

Get out of debt. File bankruptcy if you need to, knowing that shame is now a non-issue. Find a good financial advisor, invest some money, and get wise advice and counsel. Women are great at math and money. We must take ownership and responsibility for our financial literacy and prowess, and be sure to pass it on. Leave a legacy. At the very least, empower the next generation to do so.

Know what you want and ask for it. Negotiate, but don't settle. Share your genius. If you can't be honest, it's not real. It's better to argue than live with false peace. Embrace your sensuality and sexuality. It's a part of who you are too. Dance by yourself and get comfortable letting the music move you. Try dancing to only what you hear in your spirit. It's a part of who you are. Get in touch with your body. Love it and all of its imperfections. Volunteer. Serve. Give back. The world is greater when we share.

Believe in love and the greater good. Don't ignore evil, but don't give it any energy to make it more than what it is. Love fiercely and with abandon. Fail forward. Regret and shame are overrated, so don't traffic in them.

CHAPTER 5

Midlife Money Matters

*"I had to make my own living and my own opportunity.
But I made it! Don't sit down and wait for the
opportunities to come. Get up and make them."*
— *Madam C. J. Walker*

As I navigate this midlife terrain, I've discovered that the area that gives me the most pause and angst is money. I mean, I'm concerned about my paunch and thinning hair, but not as much as I am about my second-half-of-life money situation. It's that same kind of WTH? you experience when you look back over your life and think you should've accomplished more by now. Except it's, "I definitely should have more money than this by now. WTH?" Well, you can't have more money if you didn't make more money and if you didn't make more money, you can't save more money. It's as simple as that. The question is why not?

I realized that I've never had a conversation with anyone in my family about money. Not a one. The Brown women—my grandmother, mother, and all of my aunts-taught me that you work hard and honestly and pay your bills. But the only actual dialogue I ever had was when my mother told me to "Take this check over to the rental office." It's funny, but it's true.

The only other direction I was given was in church concerning tithing. It wasn't really a conversation per se, but the song at offering time said, "bring ye all the tithes into the storehouse." I was taught that it's important to honor God with the first fruits of your bounty. I always did and I always do. I believe in it, period. It's how my faith is set up. It's what I did or didn't do with the other 90% that has me shook.

Statistics about the pay and wealth gap for African-Americans and African-American women in particular are staggering and they're only getting worse. Systemic racism and sexism are alive and well, and make the modicum of success we do have a testament to our brilliance. It's like we've been fighting with one hand tied behind our backs and we're still managing to win.

Notwithstanding, I don't want to dismiss the fact that there are plenty of sisters getting their paper and helping and educating others to do the same. The number of African-American women entrepreneurs is outpacing other groups and it's a praise-worthy achievement. I'm so proud, but it really is a drop in the bucket. I encountered a comment from a millennial that keeps resonating in my spirit: "The issue is not just the wealth gap, but a financial literacy gap. Knowing can make the difference." Amen.

When you're woefully financially illiterate and you realize that retirement is less than a generation away, and you're not prepared, that's frightening to say the least. Statistics show that most Baby Boomers aren't prepared. Add to that taking care of aging parents and still propping up adult children, and you have a recipe for hysteria. I hear what some of you are thinking: "But you have a husband. Doesn't he take care of you?" Yes, I have a husband and he's a damn good one. However, my inward journey revealed to me that I was too dependent on him. The truth of the matter is, I'm the one responsible for my financial health and status.

Let me bust up all your bubbles. Being married is not inoculation from financial ruin or responsibility. You *both* need to make sure you have a plan to protect one another and that each of you are prepared for your future. The vows say, "Til death do us part," so we must be prepared if that happens. Feigning ignorance will never get the bills paid. As women of a certain age, we're way beyond someone taking care of us. Marriage is a partnership and you'd better be able to stand in your own stilettos or flats or whatever floats your boat. The point is, you command your own financial agency. It's a hard but necessary lesson for all women.

Once I emerged from my financial stupor, I started downloading e-books, listening to podcasts, dusting off my dreams and saying, "God, please redeem the time." One of my favorite books is *You Are a Bad**s at Making Money: Master the Mindset of Wealth* , by Jen Sincero. It was just the kick in the tush I needed. Since money is neutral and not the culprit, I realized that I had to deal with my emotional behavior and beliefs related to finances. As I continued to do the self-work, the Spirit kept connecting the dots and leading me to the information I needed to push forward.

What I know is it's all connected—head, heart, and hand. I am determined to live whole and that includes my purse. My purpose on Earth is to reflect God and help others do the same. It may look different at different seasons in my life, but I know that as I walk boldly in it, wealth will come as I trust God and do the work. Just like power and love is within, so is my wealth.

It's not too late to gain the financial wisdom and acumen you need to help you flourish in midlife and beyond. It won't be easy, but it's necessary and worth it. I'm a work in progress and I'm excited about my future. If you're less than enamored with your midlife financial situation, do the work. Google, go to the library, see a therapist, read some books, take some classes, or join a support group. Whatever you do, don't make it anyone else's responsibility. When you come through—and you will, help another sister out. My midlife money mantra is: "I'm no longer stressing, I'm manifesting!"

INSPIRATION FOR
ENLIGHTENED WOMEN

CHAPTER 6

Ditch The Fear

"When I dare to be powerful – to use my strength in the service of my vision, then it becomes less and less important whether I am afraid."
— Audre Lorde

Showing up in your own life every day is a challenge. Although you may be up, dressed, meeting needs, being a captain of industry, and tending to your daily responsibilities, you still may not be showing up in life. Your goal is to be present—not just functioning. Making each day special, not waiting for a grand holiday to embrace the moments that you're given.

We tend to dismiss the opportunity to find the divine and special in the ordinary. When we do, we miss a lot because the ordinary adds up to an extraordinary life. The daily commute to work can be ho-hum, even frustrating, but what if you create a soundtrack of your favorite tunes and sing along on the way? Be intentional about being purposeful. I'm not saying you have to jump out of an airplane, unless you want to, but I am saying don't be afraid to sit with yourself for a few moments each day, enjoying your own company.

Do something today that will bring you genuine joy. Don't worry about seeming self-centered. You are the center and everything else emanates from you. Living is not about what you have or what you've accomplished. It's about doing the things that matter most and not postponing your basic right to happiness because life has gotten in the way. Tomorrow isn't promised to any of us. Make the most of your time on Earth. Ditch the fear and live.

What can you do right now that will bring you joy?

_____

_____

_____

_____

_____

_____

_____

_____

_____

Enlightened Inspiration:

I choose to live and be present in my life today.

Here's the thing, life is going to change around you and time is going to move on with or without you. Are you going to allow your-self to grow and evolve into the best, happiest and most fulfilled you possible? Every experience, from the traumatic to the joyful, teaches us who we are and what's inside our hearts. You shouldn't be the same at 50 as you were at 40. It's your divine right to grow, evolve, change, and live. Give in to your evolution. You are not your past. Release it as a part of your life and know your best days are ahead of you.

Learn from the past, but don't live there. Embrace your becoming, and in the meantime, just be. Don't let your circumstances dictate the trajectory of your life. Assess your mental and emotional health often to determine if you're evolving into a stronger and wiser self or if you're shrinking and stuck. If you feel like you're in the latter category, don't give up hope. The opportunity to change is always ahead of you. You make no progress when you fight the inevitability of change. Not just change, but often change in the midst of difficult circumstances.

*What past experience do you need to
extract a lesson from and then release?*

_____

_____

_____

_____

_____

_____

_____

_____

_____

Enlightened Inspiration:

I am not my experiences. I learn and grow from them.
They all create the mosaic that is my ever-evolving and
interesting life.

It's not too late to start again and become the woman your heart said you were all along. Sometimes we take the wisdom of a new day for granted. The sun, moon and stars know the joy of starting over and don't try to stay in place beyond their allotted times. They've all been divinely designed with an innate timing and wisdom to fully be what the Creator intended. Because we are the pinnacle of creation, that universal truth is available to us too.

Each sunrise is the opportunity for a new beginning, but that's easy to overlook when life takes unexpected turns. Those vicissitudes can make us forget what we know to be true about ourselves and our reason for existing. Newsflash—you can begin again. Start with that thought and you'll discover that the dream you had for yourself is still waiting to be lived. Or better yet, you may even dream a new dream!

Enlightened Inspiration:

*"Birds flying high, you know how I feel. Sun in the sky, you
know how I feel. Breeze drifting on by, you know how I
feel. It's a new dawn, it's a new day, it's a new life for me.
And I'm feeling good."*
— *Nina Simone*

It's never too late to take your passion off the shelf and dust
it off. Look at the sun and moon, and be reminded that you pos-
sess the same wisdom and intellect to live beyond your yester-
days. Become what your heart has been whispering for you to
believe you could be—free, whole and rejoicing in each new day.

*If you could breathe life into a put-aside dream,
which one would you revive?*

_____

_____

_____

_____

_____

_____

_____

_____

CHAPTER 7

Sacred Sisterhood

*"Is solace anywhere more comforting than
that in the arms of a sister?"*
— *Alice Walker*

You can't do life by yourself. It's okay to be vulnerable and ask for help. It's okay to lean on someone else in times of difficulty. The stereotypes of Black woman rugged individualism and the superwoman identity are myths. There's nothing super about telling yourself you don't need help or anybody else. God didn't need help, but clearly knew that man did. So a woman was created—yes, it was the best idea ever!

Humans were never meant to carry the load of life alone. Maybe you think you're superhuman, but even God decided to do things in community, as in Father, Son and Holy Spirit. Jesus had numerous disciples, at one time, as many as 70. He was selective about his inner circle and we should be too. There's joy in being part of an intimate group of confidantes, truth-tellers, tear-wipers, joke-getters, secret-sharers and gut-busting laugh partners to share our lives and loads.

There's a difference between being alone and being lonely. Vulnerability is a strength and it's just plain good sense to acknowledge that we don't have all of the answers. With the exception of "I love you," the three most powerful words we can say are "I need help."

Enlightened Inspiration:

I am strongest when I admit I don't have it all under control. There is beauty in my vulnerability. My wisdom allows me to seek support and assistance when I can't go any further in my own strength. Shame and guilt are non-issues. I am never alone, and I am not the only one with struggles and difficulty. When I am weak, that's when I am strong. God's strength is made perfect in my weakness. Sisterhood is God's way of giving you someone to celebrate your strengths and cover your weaknesses because another woman can see herself in you.

Have you bought into the superwoman myth?
If so, how?

_____

_____

_____

_____

_____

_____

_____

_____

_____

Has it served you well? If not, what steps will you take to get the support and help you need in a difficult area of your life?

_____

_____

_____

_____

_____

_____

_____

_____

Sometimes there are no words to explain the kinship and sacred trust between women friends. The laughter, the silence, the looks, the embraces, the fierce protection, the advice, whether solicited or not, the pushes, the pulls, the tears, the pain, the you, the me, the divine connection, the ride or die—it's all magical and often serendipitous. It can be painful when motives are tested and jealousies arise, but a good sister-friend is worth fighting for, not just fighting with. Really look into your sister's eyes and when you embrace her, hold her with care and love because you are seeing and embracing yourself.

Enlightened Inspiration:

Sacred sisterhood is a divine idea and a necessity for my soul. I will try to create a mutually beneficial and safe place for my sister because my sister is me.
You deserve God's best because you are here. Your existence is God's approval.

What makes a good sister-friend?

_____

_____

_____

_____

_____

_____

_____

_____

_____

Are you a good sister-friend? In what way
can you show yourself sisterly?

_____

_____

_____

_____

_____

_____

_____

_____

_____

Think of 3-5 sister-friends and say a prayer for them or call them to express how they have added to the quality of your life.

_____

_____

_____

_____

_____

_____

_____

_____

_____

CHAPTER 8

Take Charge

"You can't be hesitant about who you are."
— *Viola Davis*

Giving away your power and ability to make your own life choices for your own happiness is one of the most unfortunate things that can happen to you. When you put everyone else's dreams and desires above your own, you cause the slow death of your physical vitality and spirit. In other words, you will become the walking dead. You can restore yourself when you own your power and choices. That starts with what you believe about yourself. You have to believe your happiness, joy, and self-actualization is a birthright. It's not optional and non-negotiable.

Take an inventory of what's missing in your life.
How will you reclaim it?

_____

_____

_____

_____

_____

_____

_____

_____

_____

What do you really believe about yourself?

_____

_____

_____

_____

_____

_____

_____

_____

Enlightened Inspiration:

Your power is within.

We will never know our greatest potential or sweetest relationship if we subconsciously believe we're undeserving of all the joy and fulfillment life has to offer. Self-sabotage is rooted in a subterranean belief that we don't belong, fit in or measure up to others. Seeking approval and acceptance from people who really don't have it to give is like a dog chasing its tail. No one can give you your self-worth or ability to believe in yourself. You were born with it.

Every human being deserves to be honored and treated with respect and love without condition. We were born free and loved, and when we encounter anything less, it diminishes our spirit and our true self. Remember, the Creator said, "Let there be you" and you were. That is enough.

Do you struggle with complete acceptance of yourself?

_____

_____

_____

_____

_____

_____

_____

_____

Name three reasons why the world needs your presence:

_____

_____

_____

_____

_____

_____

_____

_____

Enlightened Inspiration:

Write a self-affirmation to remind yourself how wonderful you are and thank the Creator for making you _____ (you fill in the blank!)

_____

_____

_____

_____

_____

_____

_____

_____

_____

CHAPTER 9

Stay The Course

"It's not the load that breaks you down,
it's the way you carry it."
— Lena Horne

D on't give up. The struggle is necessary because life requires endurance. If you're under the impression that
life is supposed to be easy and you think you're doing
something wrong because you're facing difficulties, let me tell
you a secret—life is not life without difficulties.

Of course, we're not supposed to go out of our way to invite
challenges into our lives, but they will arise. Since they're inevitable, the dilemma is deciding how you will navigate them. How
will they change you? For good or for bad? Will they cause you
to stumble and have a meltdown or go inward for strength? Cry,
scream, rant, rave, get therapy, take a trip, do whatever you need
to do. Just don't give up.

Each triumph makes you stronger because it shows you
what you're made of—God strength. Endure because life is a

marathon, not a sprint. You have a few more laps to go, so make them good and make them count. Someone is in the stands watching your race but there's also someone in the stands cheering you on to victory.

Think of a particular struggle or challenge.
What's your perspective of it?
What meaning have you given it?

_____

_____

_____

_____

_____

_____

_____

_____

How are you learning to endure?

_____

_____

_____

_____

_____

_____

_____

_____

_____

What strengths and wisdom have you gained from overcoming a difficult point or season in your life?

_____

_____

_____

_____

_____

_____

_____

_____

Enlightened Inspiration:

Quitting is not an option. I will not give up on myself.
Difficult and challenging times, even loss and feeling lost,
are part of my journey. Weeping may endure for a night,
but joy will come in the morning and I get to determine
when morning comes. If the night seems to be more than
I can handle, I will reach out to others on the journey to
walk with me, run with me, even carry me, if necessary.
But I won't give up.

Beautiful Brokenness

I don't believe gratuitous suffering makes us better or more holy or more honorable. I also don't think the narrative that celebrates the long-suffering of women in untenable and spirit-breaking relationships makes us more devoted or ride or die, especially when there's no expectation of change.

I do know, however, that life can be complex, unpredictable, and painful. Our spirits will encounter people who aren't yet acquainted with the gift of love, and their lack of emotional knowledge can inflict brokenness on others. We're told that we're supposed to be strong, but our silent cries and unseen pain plague us, and they can't be assuaged by a fierce hairdo, designer wardrobe or Ruby Woo-adorned smiles.

One of the connecting points of humanity is that we've all felt abandoned and alone at some time. This is also the connecting point to God, who transforms hurt into a measure of strength you didn't know you had. If you don't deal with your pain, it will deal with you. Your store of strength is for you when you need it and for sisters who will benefit from your tears, triumph, and testimony along the way.

We aren't beautiful because we haven't been broken. We're beautiful because we have been. And in spite of it, we've chosen to live.

I am beautiful because my pain and brokenness taught me...

_____

_____

_____

_____

_____

_____

_____

_____

Enlightened Inspiration:

*I will listen to my pain and gently tend to my brokenness.
I will be careful about who I share my pain with because
everyone is not worthy, and I will find a caring tribe
who will allow me to be vulnerable and cheer me on as I
conquer the world.
Just because it's not easy doesn't mean it's not worth it!*

I could tell you, "Sister, go for your dreams. It will be well. It's a piece of cake!" Except I'd be lying through my teeth. The truth is, many times it will not be well and it'll be hard as hell. That doesn't mean you aren't supposed to take a leap of faith and fall in love, get counseling, end the relationship, start a family, launch a business, move to another city, join a church, buy a home, write a book, change careers or just be you.

Difficulties and failures are not a sign that you need to quit. They just mean you need to regroup and let go of the notion that if it's true and it's God-ordained, it's not supposed to be hard. No one has ever achieved anything great without experiencing great heartache along the way. Hardships are a motive purifier and gateway to self-awareness. That's really what this journey is about—remembering who we really are and what's important. God doesn't give us dreams to fulfill just for us to shine. The journey is intended to refine us and make us become everything She envisioned before we took our first breath.

So don't give up. You reflect the Divine. Take a beat. Breathe. Lean on your tribe. Adjust your crown and keep moving. Your life is an answered prayer and everything you have to overcome to live it and step into your dreams will be so worth it.

I almost gave up because...

_____

_____

_____

_____

_____

_____

_____

_____

_____

I can't give up because...

_____

_____

_____

_____

_____

_____

_____

_____

Enlightened Inspiration:

The struggle will strengthen me if I don't let it break me.

CHAPTER 10

The Power Of Love

"Just remember the world is not a playground but a schoolroom. Life is not a holiday but an education. One eternal lesson for us all: to teach us how better we should love."
—Barbara Jordan

First Peter 4:8 says, "—and above all things have fervent love for one another, for love covers a multitude of sins."[1] Love doesn't excuse failings and shortcomings nor does it dismiss them. Love covers them. It makes room for them and allows missteps and mistakes. Sin is not the symptomatic behavior we all hide behind. Existing short of God's desired fullness and best for us because we don't believe we're loved—that is sin.

---

[1] 1 Peter 4:8 (NKJV)

Let love in. It's greater than we have allowed it to be. As the songwriter Hal David and composer Burt Bacharach said, "What the world needs now is love, sweet love. It's the only thing that there's just too little of."

If we're not living in love, we're living in fear, and fear can drive us to unhealthy habits and behaviors. Love without conditions breeds confidence, security, health, ambition and joy. But we have somehow convinced ourselves that love is not enough, so we won't completely surrender to its inspiring, healing power. Instead, we resort to manipulation, control, and games.

And it all begins with self-love. The starting point to love is not the other, it is self. We often cling to our love for others like a life raft in the middle of the ocean. It becomes the substitute for loving ourselves. That's like feeding someone else and expecting to get nourished and full. When we do this our soul will always go wanting because that is too much to expect from another frail human being. Divine self-love innoculates you from loving others for the wrong reason. When you love yourself, you love others from a place of divine strength. That's the power of love.

Do you believe in love?

_____

_____

_____

_____

_____

_____

_____

_____

What is love to you?

_____

_____

_____

_____

_____

_____

_____

_____

_____

What belief do you need to surrender so you can receive and give love unconditionally?

_____

_____

_____

_____

_____

_____

_____

_____

Enlightened Inspiration:

Love is the greatest power in the universe. The Creator is love and I am love, made from love, to love. I open my heart to receive and give non-judging love to others. When I feel fear, I will ask my Creator to help me return to love.

Love on You

This was one of the harder entries for me to write. I checked in with God to make sure I had to do it and She answered me with, "What did I say?" If you know like I know, that means "Don't ask me again. Do what I said!" Confession is supposed to be good for the soul, so here it is.

It took me a very long time to stop comparing my life and accomplishments to other peoples' and stop waiting for perfection before I started loving and celebrating myself. I've learned that perfection is an illusion and comparison is the devil. Together, they're a recipe for perpetual disappointment and depression.

You don't need permission to know and love yourself. You also don't need to be like anyone else to be happy. People get paid millions of dollars to make you unsatisfied with yourself and your life, but don't fall for it. Develop your own standard of being based on these words: "And God said it was good." You were created in the image of God. Your very being and the body that houses it are covered with a big divine YAAAASSSSS!

We will never have true joy and freedom if we don't embrace self-love and self-acceptance. Love the you that you are right now, even if you know you need and want to make changes that will improve your quality of life. Anything that is not rooted in love won't last and if you're trying to be something you're not—motivated by the need to be accepted, affirmed or approved by other flawed human beings, you'll be sorely disappointed and your soul will be left wanting more.

I finally got it. I'm right where I'm supposed to be, being who I'm supposed to be. Throughout my adventurous midlife madness and magnificence, I'm loving the me I've become on this leg of my unique journey. You will grow and evolve, as we all should, and while you do, love yourself each step of the way. Love you on your way to you. It makes the journey divine.

List as many qualities that you love about yourself as you can. Then have a party to celebrate the rebirth of you.

Enlightened Inspiration:

You are God's divine creation. You are already loved.

CHAPTER 11

Live Your Truth

"What I know for sure is that you feel real joy in direct proportion to how connected you are to living your truth."
— *Oprah Winfrey*

Once you know your truth, live your truth. Take time to learn what's sacred to you and no one will be able to disturb your peace. Truth can be very subjective. As a matter of fact, truth is simply what you believe to be so. One person's truth can be someone else's lie. In other words, your truth is your reality. The trouble with that is sometimes it's the result of experiences and conclusions that may not be life-affirming or life-giving. The truth that we espouse and live with may actually be a survival technique.

There's transcendent truth in the wholeness of God, and it reflects your beauty, sacredness, and uniqueness. Your right to your own thoughts. Freedom to create your desired environments. Release from the tyranny of the "shoulds." Woman, know thyself.

When you live your sacred truth, you honor who you are and your peace will prevail through life's storms.

Whose life are you living?

_____

_____

_____

_____

_____

_____

_____

_____

_____

Whose thoughts are you thinking?

_____

_____

_____

_____

_____

_____

_____

_____

_____

What is sacred to you about you?

_____

_____

_____

_____

_____

_____

_____

_____

What do you know is true about and for you?

_____

_____

_____

_____

_____

_____

_____

_____

Enlightened Inspiration:

I know and live my own truth. If my life doesn't afford me joy and freedom, I must align with ultimate truth to achieve the love and peace of knowing my worth. That doesn't mean anyone else has to live my truth. But I won't accept and bring into my sacred space anyone who attempts to disturb my peace by projecting their truth onto me. Walking in my own truth and allowing others to do the same makes me a peace-maker. Therefore, I am blessed.

CHAPTER 12

Midlife: A Radical Reset

Midlife requires a radical reset, a reboot of sorts. It marks the transition from one state of being into another, except there's no midlife womanhood training, manuals, celebration or naming ceremony. Midlife is a shift, a transformation, a rebirth, a becoming. It's dynamic and fluid. Midlife isn't a person, place or thing, yet it has its own characteristic traits and telltale signs. Ultimately, it's a very personal and unique experience for every woman.

It can be especially harrowing for women because there are so many myths to decry and so much gender conditioning to abandon. For African-American women there's even more to overcome. Dismantling the protective armor that shielded us from the negativity and oppression. Embracing the skin, the hair, the bodies, the souls, the spirits we were conditioned to reject. It's a wonder we made it to midlife at all even battered and bruised. We made it because we are fierce warrior women. Like Jacob in the Bible, we're ready to wrestle with ourselves and come out victorious, new names and all. It's a process of accepting and rejecting truth and lies at the same time.

Midlife is a season of radicalization because we are no longer willing to fit into a prescribed box. We are coloring outside the lines and jaywalking into a new existence. Warning—all this fierceness comes with some sacrifices and side-effects. Your relationships will have to be redefined, and you may endure painful losses. You will also celebrate some unexpected gains. Midlife is an experience, a tumultuous journey that, if traveled well, will lead to sacred serenity. Should you choose to embrace the metamorphosis, your spirit, mind, body and soul will thank you for making peace with yourself.

It's difficult to define midlife because the timing is fluid, although it's generally when you begin to experience the symptoms of perimenopause, which could be anywhere from ages 35-45. The symptoms aren't just biological, they're spiritual and psychological as well and they work in tandem, which is why the shift can be so overwhelming. Our body, mind, spirit, and soul seem to be experiencing an upheaval all at the same time. You may not always be able to articulate what you're experiencing, and if you're like me, you may even forget in mid-sentence, but your entire being is experiencing the change.

Since women have often been told to stay quiet and keep yourself to yourself, we suffer in silence and miss the opportunity to flourish and evolve in community. Our response often creates more harm than good. We've been so estranged from the ancient wisdom of our ancestors that by the time we acknowledge the changes we are experiencing, they seem more like a crisis. That denotes a loss of control. So let's reframe it as a midlife "becoming."

I choose to create the narrative that in midlife, I am rediscovering the joy of being me. Exploring and expanding to embrace both the messiness and magnificence of midlife. Ultimately maturing to master them both. Honoring the joys and sorrows of life as par for the course. My life experiences are not my identity — they are only proof that I'm alive and I get to choose what meaning they carry. In midlife, I count my blessings and cut my losses. I'm being reborn, except this time I'm giving birth to myself and the Holy Spirit is my midlife midwife.

Can this really be done? Yes, it can. As we navigate this season of disequilibrium, it helps to know that your spirit is really telling you it's time to live a life of meaning and fulfillment, a life of saying "yes" to yourself. It's time to do the work to know who you really are, not who you are expected to be. It's time to go inward to discover what you really want to do, not what you are expected to do. It's time to figure out what you want, not just what everyone else wants. It's time to unleash your potential and soar. To be clear, I'm not offering you a quick fix, an easy answer or a formula. I'm inviting you to take a step into the unknown known to reflect, remember, release, reclaim and rejoice.

Reflect

Be intentional about committing time to reflect on your life. Where have you been? Which experiences and people have had the most impact on you? What words and feelings created the narrative that created your life? Who are you—really? Not who you want to be, but who are you now? Not the "who" someone told you that you had to be, who are you without their influence? You can't authentically offer yourself to love and to the world until you know who you are.

When I got tired of hitting the wall, I realized that I had to go within. I had to ask myself some hard questions and I was finally ready to answer. My experience of fatherlessness created fear and unworthiness. I was afraid of loss, rejection, and abandonment. I lacked the confidence to go beyond a certain level. I wasn't hidden. I was hiding.

Many women are the walking dead because they refuse to look at their life and learn from it. We've been taught to keep it moving and ignore what we're feeling, many of us get stuck and only respond to the world with anger and fear. Both are only secondary emotions. The primary emotions—the real emotions are usually the pain and hurt of rejection, disappointment, and abandonment.

Let's face it—if you're not growing, you're dying. Reflection is a gift of grace and mercy, and a springboard to personal growth. It's a spiritual discipline that requires us to slow down and feel. It allows you to look back on a moment or a season or an accomplishment to identify where you are as a result. Do I need to mourn? Do I need to celebrate? Do I need to adjust? Where do I go from here? Embrace the lessons and make a declaration to change. Then move forward. Leave the timing up to the Holy Spirit and sometimes a good girlfriend who is willing to say "Okay, that's enough of that."

Don't strive for the outward appearance of success and achievement at the expense of your mental and emotional health. Accomplishments aside, you have to know who you really are. Reflection helps you get to know yourself and your motivations. Accomplishments should be related to your purpose and life fulfillment, not to prove that you are worthy. The negative emotions I discovered weren't the totality of who I was, but it was the underlying truth that guided how I showed up or didn't show up in the world for others and myself.

My midlife messiness forced me to embrace the practice of reflection. I discovered that when I did I could move beyond self-imposed limitations. I also discovered that I should be proud of who I was and what I accomplished despite that handicap. It's all a part of my human story of resilience. If you take the time to reflect and honor your life, what will you discover?

Remember

It's normal to feel lost in midlife. It's the lingering in the unsettling space of who you no longer are and who you have yet to become. We often wonder if what we're doing matters. We feel off-kilter, but can't really identify the reason why. It's a general feeling of malaise. It's as if we have been suffering from a slow leak of our joy and zeal. Sometimes we're also filled with regret, even anger, and then guilt for feeling regret and anger. The trifecta of those specific emotions can rob you of your optimism and hope.

You're not alone. The first time I realized that I had no idea who the artists on an award show were, the first time I needed to take a class at the Apple store with a real person because I couldn't grasp the tutorial online, and the first time I heard myself say, "Y'all need to stop all of that texting and pick up the phone," I thought, it's over. I'm officially irrelevant.

When you start thinking that your best days are behind you or your dreams and ideas will never happen, it's time to remember the core of who you are — free, fun, fearless and willing to try new things. Untainted by heartbreak and disappointment. Full of promise and potential. Uninhibited. I didn't say everything was perfect. But then again, it doesn't have to be. Remember the level of imagination and creativity you had to pour into making something work just because you really wanted it to? The best of who you are is still who you are!

I will never forget the impact of a sermon by Dr. Jasmin Scularkk, better known as "Dr. Jazz," titled "I Remember Me." Whew, can I tell you how that thing shook some stuff loose?

Remember the power you had before you gave it away? Your spirit hasn't forgotten who you are and who God says you are. Loved. Whole. Worthy. Powerful. Gifted. Dr. Jazz said, "Jesus didn't just want to be remembered for what He did, but who He was. He wasn't just admonishing the disciples to honor the first communion, "do this in remembrance of me," but to recall His smile, His compassion, His strength. Him. He was a person, both human, and divine, and so are you.

Get in the presence of God, the One who created you, to jog your memory about who you really are. On her podcast, "Coming Home," Dr. Thema Bryant teaches on the Swahili concept of "kujua," which means "remembering what you already know." Your spirit knows how amazing you still are and that your latter will be greater than your former. You are beautiful, brilliant, and capable. You just need to remember it.

Release

Midlife is the perfect time to release people, habits, thoughts, ideas, pain and blame. Even if you're the one who messed up, release it. The world encourages us to hold on to dreams, but be free to release those that no longer fit you. If it doesn't work out, let it go. Nothing ever really belongs to us anyway, even our dreams. God gives us our ideas for the good of humanity. When we try to hold on too tightly, we begin to take on unhealthy ownership and unhealthy burdens. Remember the episode of

"A Different World" when Whitley Gilbert said, "Relax, relate, release?" Give yourself permission to do that.

Take an assessment of your goals, vision, relationships, and the interior elements of your life. Ask yourself: is this working for me? Is it beneficial? Is it part of my life mission? Does it bring me joy?

Sometimes you can't pinpoint negative energy because it's unseen, but it's definitely felt. Trust your gut. Cleaning clears the energy. Maybe you need to clean your house and throw some things away, both physically and metaphorically. Release emotions that have been caught up in your body. Take a deep breath and exhale with sound. Do it two or three times. Move your body to release pent-up emotions. Many of us have been to the doctor to see about a pain or an icky feeling a gazillion times only to hear them say over and over again that you're fine. The problem could be that your body is registering emotions you haven't dealt with. Go ahead and cry. Work out your anger and frustrations at a boxing gym. Release your old life so you can embrace the new one.

Honor your life and know that nothing is ever wasted. Embrace difficult seasons as a part of your story and shift the balance of power. Once I was able to reflect and come to terms with the emotional culprit in my life, I had to resolve that it was no longer going to rule me. I had to remember who I was and how far I had come. Then I released the old narrative and exchanged it for a more empowering one.

That doesn't mean everything you release is a one and done. You may have to let go of a thought or feeling more than once. The key is you're now more self-aware. It's like meditation. A thought may emerge and try to hijack your focus, but just acknowledge it, let it float by and return to your center.Do it as many times as you need to and before you know it, you've tamed your monkey mind.

Reclaim

It's time to get your life back. I'm not saying what you've been doing with your life isn't worthwhile, or even admirable, but know that it's okay to shift gears. It's okay to change careers, right-size your life, shift priorities and close "The Bank of You," so you can focus on your financial future.

It's not my intent to over-generalize, but women have often been taught to be self-sacrificing to a fault, and put our own needs and desires on the back burner for our significant others, children, grand-children, employers, organizations, churches, parents and the planet. You name it, we can sacrifice for it.

Now be clear, I know that situations and seasons call for sacrifice, like taking care of aging or ailing spouses, children and parents, or raising grandchildren because their parents can't rise to the occasion. But you are not required to prove your strength, worth or commitment by doing it all by yourself, endangering your health and wellbeing in the effort. Don't let others guilt you into doing so. Often caregivers become ill themselves, and at worst, leave this Earth before the people under their care. There's help and support. Reclaim yourself, your time, and your mental health.

In 2017, Congresswoman Maxine Waters famously stated during a Congressional hearing, "I'm reclaiming my time." Each committee member has an allotted number of minutes to question the person testifying before them and apparently someone was taking up too much of her time with superfluous nonsense. She repeated the phrase "reclaiming my time" until the testifier stopped talking and the chairman recognized her declaration and gave her time back and made the person answer her question. Rep. Waters was successful in her request because she knew the rules and spoke out on her own behalf. It's time all midlife women do the same.

It doesn't matter how long you have given up your agency, let others run over you or run off with your priorities. Once you come to yourself and you're ready to reclaim yourself, speak up. Know the rules of life engagement and stand on them. You have a right to your peace of mind. Declare that you will no longer allow others to make their procrastination your emergency. Declare that your money is yours to decide to keep or share, but everyone attached to you is not entitled to it.

Your ideas and creative license are yours, and you don't have to continue to share them without compensation. You are entitled to change your mind and speak your mind. You have the right to do things that make you happy and you don't owe anyone an explanation. Most men very rarely explain their actions or need co-signers. They just do it and expect support. Matter of fact, they get offended if you don't contort yourself to give it.

In midlife, if I hold things in too long, my body begins to rebel. I feel ill and depressed. So I speak to the wounded me and remind her that the whole me can handle it, and I share what I need to share and let the chips fall where they may. I'm not reckless. I'm responsible with my words, but I'm no longer as careful as I once was. Being too careful diminished my soul. Take courage and reclaim yourself to reclaim your life. The world is waiting for the *real* you.

Rejoice

Look in the mirror and smile at yourself. Don't focus on what you think is wrong or need to improve. Look deep into your own eyes and tell yourself thank you. Thank you for surviving. Thank you for the times you wanted to give up, but you found a way to start over again and didn't give up on yourself. Let that smile turn into a full-blown grin for all of the times that people said you weren't going to make it or told you no. You kept believing and pushing. Get downright giddy about the fact that you were brave enough to love, again and again—and that you are finally learning to love yourself. Let yourself feel the joy. Rejoice!

Rejoicing is not the same as celebrating. A celebration is the tangible result of rejoicing. The word "rejoice" is an intransitive verb meaning "to feel joy or great delight." It's a feeling, an emotion. It's not something directed at, for or to anyone or anything else. It's something that's within that allows you to honor your being. It means to feel content with yourself. That means it's extremely important to have good thoughts about yourself. How you think determines how you feel, and how you feel is the true impetus behind how you act and the decisions that you make.

Allow yourself to feel joy. It's the by-product of taking the time to reflect, remember, release, and reclaim your worth and your power. It's the power of embracing yourself- all of yourself, including your quirks, proclivities, strengths and weaknesses and still finding your greatness. It's knowing that your journey has brought you to a place of knowing. It is knowing that your journey to self is more about being at peace than doing anything else. Joy is realizing that God meant what She said when She declared as you were being knit in your mother's womb, "......and she is good."

I complete this reflection with tears welling up in my eyes at the realization that my Creator-God has long been wooing and pulling me to this place of acceptance. My brain, body and spirit had to come into alignment with the wisdom of time. I have not completed my journey, but I am acknowledging that I am complete in God. I don't have to strive to prove my beautifully divine humanity. I only have to embrace it.

I don't have to wait for something to happen to feel joy. I feel it when the sun warms my face. I feel it when a cool breeze chills my bones. I feel it when I breathe, knowing that I am still alive. I feel it when I write. I feel it when I share my soul. I feel it when I embrace my sister co-journer. I feel it in the presence of the Holy. My joy isn't a shield from the vicissitudes of life. It is my hope, light, and anchor in the midst of them.

Our joy is why we sorrow. Sorrow isn't the antithesis of joy—it is the sister of it. We need both to be fully human. Don't let it make you afraid to rejoice. Midlife is about embracing both and knowing that you have a whole lot of life to live and rejoicing to do.

I don't want to mislead you. Finding this joy wasn't easy for me. I had to excavate. I had to dig beneath the surface. I had to acknowledge what was lost, and muster up the courage to search for it. I had to love myself enough to do the work of self-discovery and recovery. I had to rediscover the joy—the joy of being me. I hope you do the same.

My Midlife Manifesto

_____

_____

_____

_____

_____

_____

_____

_____

My Midlife Manifesto

_____

_____

_____

_____

_____

_____

_____

_____

_____

The Enlightened Woman

Rediscover the joy of being you...

"I don't have to wait for something to happen to feel joy. I feel it when the sun warms my face. I feel it when a cool breeze chills my bones. I feel it when I breathe, knowing that I am still alive. I feel it when I write. I feel it when I share my soul. I feel it when I embrace my sister co-journer. I feel it in the presence of the Holy."
—Dr. Kellie V. Hayes

Being an *Enlightened Woman* is about embracing the freedom to just "be." The freedom to be completely confident in who you are and who you are becoming in the sacred and significant season of midlife. The midlife rite of passage is a reminder that you are a priceless masterpiece ready to live a life of meaning and fulfillment. There is both madness and magnificence in this season, and if you embrace the opportunity to evolve and expand you will emerge with the grace to master it all.

About the Author

Rev. **Dr. Kellie V. Hayes** serves as the Executive Pastor of Real Power African Methodist Episcopal Church (formerly Hunter Memorial) in Upper Marlboro, Maryland, where her husband, the Rev. Dr. Harold B. Hayes, Jr. is the Senior Pastor. Together, they co-founded H & K Global Enterprises, Inc., a boutique business dedicated to helping people maximize their potential in life and love. She is the proud mother of three Kingdom purposed young adults, Shante, Shannon and Joshua—and she's ecstatic about being GiGi to her two precious granddaughters, Tehila and Daria.

Dr. Hayes completed her undergraduate work at Hampton University in Hampton, VA and earned both her masters of theological studies and doctorate of ministry from Wesley Theological Seminary in Washington, DC. She is a certified executive/transformation life coach and completed the Foundations in Christian Leadership Certificate Program at the Duke Divinity School. She is a proud member of the illustrious sisterhood of Delta Sigma Theta Sorority, Inc.

As CEO of Enlightened Woman Enterprises, the umbrella for LeadTech, Inc. and LifeVision Coaching and Consulting, she uses her gifts and passion for leadership development, strategic planning and organizational management to help individuals, corporations and nonprofits leverage their resources and creativity for peak performance. Her newest venture is The Serenity Experience, a perfectly curated intimate experience for women in midlife ready to master this magnificent season of their lives.

Above all, Dr. Hayes desires to honor God with her life by using the gifts she has been given to make an impact, and leave a legacy of healing and hope in her generation and the next.

".... yet who knows whether you have come to the

Kingdom for such a time as this."

Esther 4:14b (NKJV)

Resources

Introduction

Brice, Carleen Editor. *Age Ain't Nothing but a Number* Boston, MA: Beacon Press, 2003

Gaston, M.D., Marilyn Hughes and Gayle K. Porter, Psy.D. *Prime Time: The African American Woman's Complete Guide to Midlife Health and Wellness.* New York, NY: Ballantine Books, 2001 and 2012.

Scott Brown, Carolyn and Barbara S. Levy, M.D. *The Black Woman's Guide to Menopause: Doing Menopause with Heart and Soul.* Naperville, Illinois: Sourcebooks, Inc., 2003

Chapter 1

Weems, Renita J. *What Matters Most: Ten Lessons in Living Passionately from the Song of Solomon.* New York, NY: Warner Books, Inc. with Walk Worthy Press 2004

Chapter 2

Bryant, Thema. "Homesick and Disconnection from Ourselves". *The Homecoming* (Podcast Audio) July 5, 2019 www.drthema.com

Chapter 3

Kaiser, Stacy. "12 Ways to Celebrate You". Feb. 10, 2015 Article LiveHappy.com

Chapter 4

Vikki, Johnson Dr. *Soul Wealth: Finding Vision, Compassion, Authenticity, Abundance and Legacy in the Midst of Chaos.* Hollywood, FL: Pecan Tree Publishing, 2019

Song: "So Happy Being Me" by Anita Wilson, *Vintage Worship* *https://youtu.be/9RLGwYROhe4*

Chapter 5

Podcasts Redefining Wealth: Chasing Purpose Not Money with Patrice Washington

Brown Ambition with Mandi and Tiffany

The His and Her Money Show with Talaat & Tai McNeely

Sincero, Jen. *You are a Badass at Making Money: Master the Mindset of Wealth* New York, NY: Penguin Books, 2018

Twist, Lynne. *The Soul of Money: Transforming Your Relationship with Money and Life.* New York, NY: W.W. Norton & Company

Chapter 6

Bradford, Ph.D, Joy Harden. "Dealing with a Fear of Rejection". *Therapy for Black Girls (Podcast Audio)* October 2, 2019 therapyforblackgirls.com

Nina Simone singing "Feeling Good" https://youtu.be/Ff-0pHwyQ1g

Chapter 7

Browning, Joanne. *Our Savior Our Sisters Ourselves: Biblical Teaching & Reflections on Women's Relationships.* Fort Washington, MD: Journey of Faith, Inc., 2006

Weems, Renita J. *Just a Sister Away: Understanding the Timeless Connection Between Women of Today and Women in the Bible.* New York, NY: Warner Books with Walk Worthy Press, 2005

Adams, Kelsey. Identity "How Sisterhood Saved Me" February 20, 2019 Flare.com

Chapter 8

Obama, Michelle. *Becoming.* New York, NY: Crown Publishing Group, 2018

"Self-Love is the Best Love: 10 Reasons Black Women Should Learn how to Say "NO" November 1, 2018 blog.blkgrn.com

Song: Holy by Jamila Woods https://youtu.be/t3MhH2WekcY

Chapter 9

Brown-Rudd, Natalie. *Stormy Weather: 25 Lessons Learned While Weathering the Storms of Life* Bloomington, IN: WestBow Press, 2015

Chapter 10

india.arie's -"Private Party" from "Testimony: Vol. 1 Life & Relationships" https://youtu.be/NlkY4iUecM4

Song: Comparison Kills by Jonathan McReynolds https://youtu.be/f-8HL54VLLA

I Corinthians 13:1-13

Chapter 11

7 Signs You're Living Your Truth by Lauren Stahl

https://mindbodygreen.com/0-17919/7-signs-youre-living-your-truth.html#

Chapter 12

Blog post: The Blissful Mind Why You Should Make Time For Self-Reflection Catherine Beard January 14, 2018 https://the-blissfulmind.com/importance-of-self-reflection

Dr. Kellie

FOR BOOKING

GO TO

www.kellievhayes.global

or

www.enlightenedwoman.global

Email: kvhayes7@gmail.com

Follow Dr. Kellie on
social media outlets at

f @kellie.v.hayes   📷 @kellievhayes   🐦 @kellievhayes